Teaching Grammar with Literature

Subject and Verb Agreement with Hansel and Gretel

By
Beverly Fields
Story adapted from The brothers Grimm's Hansel and Gretel

Tempfield Press
P.O. Box 2511, Castro Valley CA 94578

Note from the Author

I am a homeschooling mom who has tried throughout my children's academic career to make learning as fun and engaging as possible. That has led me to create lots of study guides and materials over the years that incorporated more than just a textbook on each subject into their curriculum. I have also found that, often traditional text and workbooks move on to quickly for some students and don't provide additional practice for children who may not have grasped the concept right away. This lack of extra practice leads to frustration and low academic performance if students are left behind because they didn't master concepts that were part of the building blocks to bigger concepts. The constant need to keep learning fun and engaging while making sure each student has as much practice as they need to master a concept has led to this guide.

Before having my own children, and when I was just a freshman college student working as a tutor, I learned the concept of "drill and kill." When a student was having a problem with any concept we drilled it until they knew it like their own name. I was the only tutor at the agency who did not have a teaching credential and the only one who could tutor in higher math. What I found to be the biggest problem among my students was they got stuck on one concept they didn't grasp, the class moved on and they fell further behind. This is also true for language arts. Children who have language processing issues, speech and Language issues or English is not their first language suffer when they don't understand grammar. After all, no matter what subject you are taking, science, math, history, etc., the directions and reading is in English. Their writing skills fall behind because they aren't able to construct sentences properly. So, whenever I noticed students struggling I had a daily drill concept based on their needs.

Now worksheets are great for this but can be boring and actually aren't often plentiful unless you search for book after book on the subject and extract the few pages each has on the one concept your student needs. So, I decided to try and create a way for the students to engage in the material with a story concept and that provided more than enough practice for any student needing some additional practice. This guide is the result. It worked very well for my children. I hope it helps your children or students.

Teacher Note

Have students write out each sentence on the lines below each lesson. For more advanced students, introduce them to the concept of indenting.

Lesson 1: Hansel and Gretel

Directions: Choose the right word to fit the sentence.

_____

Near a thick forest **(lived, living)** a woodcutter and his wife.

They (has, had) two children.

Their daughter's name (were, was) Gretel and the son's name was Hansel.

The woodcutter (was, were) poor and had very little to eat, but they always (managing, managed.)

_____

_____

_____

_____

_____

_____

Lesson 2: Hansel and Gretel

Directions: Choose the right word(s) to fit the sentence.

_____

One day a famine befell the community and the woodcutter (couldn't, could) no longer afford to (buys, buy) his daily bread for his family.

At night he (tossing, tossed, tosses) and turned in his bed worrying about how he would (feeds, feed) his family.

"What (is, am, are) we to do? How will we (feeding, feed) our poor children when we (is unable, are unable) to feed ourselves?" he (asked, asking) his wife.

"We (will finds, will find, will finding) a way," replied his wife gently.

_____

_____

_____

_____

_____

_____

Lesson 3: Hansel and Gretel

Directions: Choose the right word to fit the sentence.

_____

The next day the woodcutter's wife, who was actually the stepmother of Hansel and Gretel, (woke, waked) the children as soon as their father left to work.

"Get up you lazy children. We must (go, going) into the forest to gather wood," she (ordered, orders).

She (give, gave) each of them a piece of bread.

"This (are, is) your dinner. Do not eat it all before then. You (wont not, will not) get any more!"

_____

_____

_____

_____

_____

_____

Lesson 4: Hansel and Gretel

Directions: Choose the right word to fit the sentence.

_____

Hansel and Gretel (believed, believes) their stepmother.

They did not (trusts, trust) her, for she (was, were) always nice and gentle with them when their father was around.

However, as soon as he was absent she (turned, turning) cruel and hard.

That morning she (ushered, ushering) them out into the woods without their father.

_____

_____

_____

_____

_____

_____

Lesson 5: Hansel and Gretel

Directions: Choose the right word to fit the sentence. Pay close attention to tense. Each option may work in the sentence but only one will be the correct tense. Ask yourself if the action is happening now, in the future or did it happen in the past.

_____

Hansel (suspects, suspected, suspecting) that she (is, was) up to something.

He thought she might try to (lose, lost) them in the forest.

He (slipped, slips) his rock collection into his pocket.

His rock collection (was, is, are) nice and shiny.

_____

_____

_____

_____

_____

_____

Lesson 6: Hansel and Gretel

Directions: Choose the right word to fit the sentence. Pay close attention to tense. Each option may work in the sentence but only one will be the correct tense. Ask yourself if the action is happening now, in the future or did it happen in the past.

_____

They (set, sat) out into the forest.

When they'd (walk, walked) a short distance, Hansel (stopped, stops) and looked back towards the house.

He (does, did) this several times more.

"What are you doing, boy?" (demands, demanded) the stepmother. "You (is, are, were) slowing us down with your lagging behind."

_____

_____

_____

_____

_____

_____

Lesson 7: Hansel and Gretel

Directions: Choose the right word to fit the sentence. Pay close attention to tense. Each option may work in the sentence but only one will be the correct tense. Ask yourself if the action is happening now, in the future or did it happen in the past.

_____

"I am sorry," replied Hansel. "I (is, am) looking at my little cat sitting on the roof."

"That (isn't not, is not) your cat, foolish boy. That is a smudge on the chimney. Come along!" the stepmother (hissed, hisses).

However, Hansel (was not, wasn't not) looking at the roof at all.

He (has been, had been) discreetly dropping one of his bright, shimmering pebbles out of his pocket onto the path.

_____

_____

_____

_____

_____

_____

Lesson 8: Hansel and Gretel

Directions: Now you will need to correct the wrong verb or action words. Put a line through the incorrect word(s) and write the correct word(s) above it. Remember to watch out for tense as well as subject verb agreement.

_____

Hansel continued to dropping the stones all through the long walk into the forest.

When they was deep into the forest the evil stepmother stops.

"This is a great place to gathered wood. Let us all go and gather what we can and met back here in an hour," she commands.

Hansel and Gretel gather wood until they had a pile as high as a little hill.

_____

_____

_____

_____

_____

_____

Lesson 9: Hansel and Gretel

Directions: Now you will need to correct the wrong verb or action words. Put a line through the incorrect word(s) and write the correct word(s) above it. Remember to watch out for tense as well as subject verb agreement.

_____

They returned in an hour to the spot they are told, but their stepmother didn't not return.

They waited until the sun begin to set.

Still, she don't return.

"I doesn't think she is coming back," Gretel cried worriedly.

_____

_____

_____

_____

_____

_____

Lesson 10: Hansel and Gretel

Directions: Now you will need to correct the wrong verb or action words. Put a line through the incorrect word(s) and write the correct word(s) above it. Remember to watch out for tense as well as subject verb agreement.

_____

"You is right, Gretel. She will not return," Hansel replies angrily.

"Then, how will we finds our way home?" Gretel asked with fearful tears running down her face.

"Just wait until the moon rises. I having a plan," Hansel reassured her.

"But, what will happened then?" Gretel asked, wipes her tears.

_____

_____

_____

_____

_____

_____

Lesson 11: Hansel and Gretel

Directions: Now you will need to correct the wrong verb or action words. Put a line through the incorrect word(s) and write the correct word(s) above it. Remember to watch out for tense as well as subject verb agreement.

_____

"We will follows the rock trail home.

I has left a trail with my shiny rocks.

They will be easier to sees when the moon are up and they reflected the moonlight."

Gretel hug her brother in relief.

_____

_____

_____

_____

_____

_____

Lesson 12: Hansel and Gretel

Directions: Now you will need to correct the wrong verb or action words. Put a line through the incorrect word(s) and write the correct word(s) above it. Remember to watch out for tense as well as subject verb agreement.

When the moon rise at last, Hansel took his sister by the hand and following the pebble path.

The rocks shone brightly in the moonlight and they founded their way home by daybreak.

"Why did you wonder into the forest," cries their stepmother. "Your father and I was worried sick."

Their father hugged them both in relief.

_____

_____

_____

_____

_____

_____

Lesson 13: Hansel and Gretel

Directions: Now you will need to correct the wrong verb or action words. Put a line through the incorrect word(s) and write the correct word(s) above it. Remember to watch out for tense as well as subject verb agreement.

_____

The next day their evil stepmother again wake them as soon as their father leave to work.

She again hands them a piece of bread and led them into the woods.

That day the bread were smaller.

Hansel no longer have his shiny rock collection, so he tear off bits of his bread and dropped them along the path.

_____

_____

_____

_____

_____

_____

Lesson 14: Hansel and Gretel

Directions: Now you will need to correct the wrong verb or action words. Put a line through the incorrect word(s) and write the correct word(s) above it. Remember to watch out for tense as well as subject verb agreement.

_____

The evil stepmother took them to a different area of the woods and orders them to gathered

wood.

They was completely unfamiliar with this area of the wood.

When they return from gathering the wood, their evil stepmother was not there and she didn't

not return.

"Did you left a trail of stones?" Gretel ask.

_____

_____

_____

_____

_____

_____

Lesson 15: Hansel and Gretel

Directions: Now you will need to correct the wrong verb or action words. Put a line through the incorrect word(s) and write the correct word(s) above it. Remember to watch out for tense as well as subject verb agreement.

_____

"No. This time I leave a trail of bread," Hansel comfort his sister.

Once the moon rose brightly, the children set out to followed the bread trail, but they find no crumbs.

Hansel quickly realize that the birds and other forest creatures must have ate the bread crumbs.

"Oh, Hansel, what will we do?" Gretel cry.

_____

_____

_____

_____

_____

_____

Lesson 16: Hansel and Gretel

Directions: Now you will need to correct the wrong verb or action words. Put a line through the incorrect word(s) and write the correct word(s) above it. Remember to watch out for tense as well as subject verb agreement.

"Don't worry, Gretel. We will found a way," Hansel replied with a confidence he did not felt.

They walking through the night and the next day also.

They still could not finds their way out of the forest.

They found nothing to ate but a few berries.

Just when they thought they could go no farther and would surely died, they come across a cottage in the woods.

Lesson 17: Hansel and Gretel

Directions: Now you will need to correct the wrong verb or action words. Put a line through the incorrect word(s) and write the correct word(s) above it. Remember to watch out for tense as well as subject verb agreement.

_____

At first they couldn't not believe their eyes.

The house appear to be made of bread and was covers with all sorts of cakes and candies.

The children was so hungry they immediately begin to pull little pieces from the house and eat them.

"Who dares to eat my home?" come a voice from within the house.

_____

_____

_____

_____

_____

_____

Lesson 18: Hansel and Gretel

Directions: Now you will need to correct the wrong verb or action words. Put a line through the incorrect word(s) and write the correct word(s) above it. Remember to watch out for tense as well as subject verb agreement.

_____

The door opens and an old lady stepped out.

"We were very sorry," the children cried. "We are lost in the woods and has not eaten. We were just so hungry."

"Oh, you poor children," the old woman said kindly. "You must are tired and hungry. Came in and I will feed you."

She took their hands and lead them into the house.

_____

_____

_____

_____

_____

Lesson 19: Hansel and Gretel

Directions: Now you will need to correct the wrong verb or action words. Put a line through the incorrect word(s) and write the correct word(s) above it. Remember to watch out for tense as well as subject verb agreement.

Then, she place platters of wonderful food in front of them.

They ate until they could not ate any more.

Then she give them soft, comfortable beds to sleep in.

The old woman were only pretending to be kind.

Lesson 20: Hansel and Gretel

Directions: Now you will need to correct the wrong verb or action words. Put a line through the incorrect word(s) and write the correct word(s) above it. Remember to watch out for tense as well as subject verb agreement.

_____

In truth, she build her candy and cake house to attract lost children.

When she capture them she would fatten them up and then eat them, for she are really a wicked witch.

The next morning the witch crept into the room and carefully pick up Hansel without waking him.

"He will be a tasty morsel," she mumble gleefully to herself.

_____

_____

_____

_____

_____

_____

Lesson 21: Hansel and Gretel

Directions: Now you will need to correct the wrong verb or action words. Put a line through the incorrect word(s) and write the correct word(s) above it. Remember to watch out for tense as well as subject verb agreement.

Gretel is a much lighter sleeper than Hansel and had awaken when the evil witch creeps into the room.

Gretel hears the witch's words and realize she plan to eat Hansel.

As soon as the witch exit the room with Hansel, Gretel quietly gets out of bed and followed her.

The witch went down some stairs and placed Hansel in a cage.

_____

_____

_____

_____

_____

_____

Lesson 22: Hansel and Gretel

Directions: Now you will need to correct the wrong verb or action words. Put a line through the incorrect word(s) and write the correct word(s) above it. Remember to watch out for tense as well as subject verb agreement.

_____

Fearing the mean witch would catch her, Gretel hurries back up the stairs and into her bed.

When the witch come to fetch her a few moments later, Gretel pretend to be asleep.

"Come, girl, and help me baking the bread for the day," the old woman ordered.

Gretel get up and followed the witch to the kitchen.

_____

_____

_____

_____

_____

_____

Lesson 23: Hansel and Gretel

Directions: Now you will need to correct the wrong verb or action words. Put a line through the incorrect word(s) and write the correct word(s) above it. Remember to watch out for tense as well as subject verb agreement.

_____

"I have already heat the stove and kneaded the dough for the bread," say the witch. "Crawl in

the oven and see if it are properly heated."

Gretel understand then that the witch intended to eat them both.

So, now she have to save herself before she could saved Hansel.

"I don't not understand. I cannot fit in there," she saying to the witch.

_____

_____

_____

_____

_____

_____

Lesson 24: Hansel and Gretel

Directions: Now you will need to correct the wrong verb or action words. Put a line through the incorrect word(s) and write the correct word(s) above it. Remember to watch out for tense as well as subject verb agreement.

_____

"Of course you can. Just squeeze right in," reply the witch.

Gretel makes a show of trying to figure out how to fit into the oven again. "No, it's is much too small."

"Silly child. Even I can fitted inside," the witch exclaimed, climbing in with inpatients to showing Gretel.

Gretel Hastily push the witch in, slammed the iron oven door and fastened the bolt.

_____

_____

_____

_____

_____

_____

Lesson 25: Hansel and Gretel

Directions: Now you will need to correct the wrong verb or action words. Put a line through the incorrect word(s) and write the correct word(s) above it. Remember to watch out for tense as well as subject verb agreement.

"Let me out!" the witch screamed, but Gretel run away to free Hansel.

She open the door leading to the lower level and running down the stairs.

She grabbed the key hanging on the wall and quickly free Hansel.

"What happen to the witch?" Hansel asks.

Lesson 26: Hansel and Gretel

Directions: Now you will need to correct the wrong verb or action words. Put a line through the incorrect word(s) and write the correct word(s) above it. Remember to watch out for tense as well as subject verb agreement. Beware. Some of the sentences may not have any errors.

"I lock her in the oven," Gretel answered.

"Let's hurry and got away from here," cried Hansel grabbing his sister's hand.

The children stop only long enough to fill their pockets and Gretel's apron with food.

Then, they fled into the forest.

_____

_____

_____

_____

_____

_____

Lesson 27: Hansel and Gretel

Directions: Now you will need to correct the wrong verb or action words. Put a line through the incorrect word(s) and write the correct word(s) above it. Remember to watch out for tense as well as subject verb agreement.

The children walk for hours and hours.

Finally they stopped to take a rest and has a bite to eat along a river bank.

"I believed I know this river," Hansel said. "I think it leads to our home."

The children set out again followed the river.

Lesson 28: Hansel and Gretel

Directions: Now you will need to correct the wrong verb or action words. Put a line through the incorrect word(s) and write the correct word(s) above it. Remember to watch out for tense as well as subject verb agreement.

_____

Sure enough, the forest began to look familiar.

And, after a long walk their house come into view.

The children ran into the house and into the arms of their father.

He cried with relief and demanding to know where they had been all of this time.

_____

_____

_____

_____

_____

_____

Lesson 29: Hansel and Gretel

Directions: Now you will need to correct the wrong verb or action words. Put a line through the incorrect word(s) and write the correct word(s) above it. Remember to watch out for tense as well as subject verb agreement.

The children told him of how they'd been lead into the forest and left behind twice.

They tell him of how they'd had found their way back the first time with the stones.

Then, they explained that the second time the birds and wild animals had eat their bread trail.

"That is curious," their father said thoughtfully, scratched his chin.

_____

_____

_____

_____

_____

_____

Lesson 30: Hansel and Gretel

Directions: Now you will need to correct the wrong verb or action words. Put a line through the incorrect word(s) and write the correct word(s) above it. Remember to watch out for tense as well as subject verb agreement.

He told them that their step mother had return home that day and bake wonderful treats that same evening.

She tells him that the children had run into the forest and she would brang them treats to try and get them to come home.

She'd baked cakes and candies and then set out with her treats to looked for them, but she never returns.

And, they never see her again.

_____

_____

_____

_____

_____

_____

Hansel and Gretel Answer Key

Lesson 1

Near a thick forest lived a woodcutter and his wife. They had two children. Their daughter's name was Gretel and the son's name was Hansel. The woodcutter was poor and had very little to eat, but they always managed.

Lesson 2

One day a famine befell the community and the woodcutter could no longer afford to buy his daily bread for his family. At night he tossed and turned in his bed worrying about how he would feed his family.

"What are we to do? How will we feed our poor children when we are unable to feed ourselves?" he asked his wife.

"We will find a way," replied his wife gently.

Lesson 3

The next day the woodcutter's wife, who was actually the stepmother of Hansel and Gretel, woke the children as soon as their father left to work.

"Get up you lazy children. We must go into the forest to gather wood," she ordered. She gave each of them a piece of bread. "This is your dinner. Do not eat it all before then. You will not get any more!"

Lesson 4

Hansel and Gretel believed their stepmother. They did not trust her for she was always nice and gentle with them when their father was around. However, as soon as he was absent she turned cruel and hard.

That morning she ushered them out into the woods without their father.

Lesson 5

Hansel suspected that she was up to something. He thought she might try to lose them in the forest. He slipped his rock collection into his pocket. His rock collection was nice and shiny.

Lesson 6

They set out into the forest. When they'd walked a short distance, Hansel stopped and looked back towards the house. He did this several times more.

"What are you doing, boy?" demanded the stepmother. "You are slowing us down with your lagging behind."

Lesson 7

"I am sorry," replied Hansel. "I am looking at my little cat sitting on the roof."

"That is not your cat, foolish boy. That is a smudge on the chimney. Come along!" the stepmother hissed.

However, Hansel was not looking at the roof at all. He had been discreetly dropping one of his bright, shimmering pebbles out of his pocket onto the path.

Lesson 8

Hansel continued to drop the stones all through the long walk into the forest.

When they were deep into the forest the evil stepmother stopped. "This is a great place to gather wood. Let us all go and gather what we can and meet back here in an hour," she commanded.

Hansel and Gretel gathered wood until they had a pile as high as a little hill.

Lesson 9

They returned in an hour to the spot they were told, but their stepmother did not return. They waited until the sun began to set. Still, she did not return.

"I don't think she is coming back," Gretel cried worriedly.

Lesson 10

"You are right, Gretel. She will not return," Hansel replied angrily.

"Then, how will we find our way home?" Gretel asked with fearful tears running down her face.

"Just wait until the moon rises. I have a plan," Hansel reassured her.

"But, what will happen then?" Gretel asked, wiping her tears.

Lesson 11

"We will follow the rock trail home. I have left a trail with my shiny rocks. They will be easier to see when the moon is up and they reflect the moonlight."

Gretel hugged her brother in relief.

Lesson 12

When the moon rose at last, Hansel took his sister by the hand and followed the pebble path. The rocks shone brightly in the moonlight and they found their way home by daybreak.

"Why did you wonder into the forest," cried their stepmother. "Your father and I were worried sick."

Their father hugged them both in relief.

Lesson 13

The next day their evil stepmother again woke them as soon as their father left to work. She again handed them a piece of bread and led them into the woods. That day the bread was smaller. Hansel no longer had his shiny rock collection, so he tore off bits of his bread and dropped them along the path.

Lesson 14

The evil stepmother took them to a different area of the woods and ordered them to gather wood. They were completely unfamiliar with this area of the wood. When they returned from gathering the wood, their evil stepmother was not there and she did not return.

"Did you leave a trail of stones?" Gretel asked.

Lesson 15

"No. This time I left a trail of bread," Hansel comforted his sister.

Once the moon rose brightly, the children set out to follow the bread trail, but they found no crumbs. Hansel quickly realized that the birds and other forest creatures must have eaten the bread crumbs.

"Oh, Hansel, what will we do?" Gretel cried.

Lesson 16

"Don't worry, Gretel. We will find a way," Hansel replied with a confidence he did not feel.

They walked through the night and the next day also. They still could not find their way out of the forest. They found nothing to eat but a few berries. Just when they thought they could go no farther and would surely die, they came across a cottage in the woods.

Lesson 17

At first they could not believe their eyes. The house appeared to be made of bread and was covered with all sorts of cakes and candies. The children were so hungry they immediately began to pull little pieces from the house and eat them.

"Who dares to eat my home?" came a voice from within the house.

Lesson 18

The door opened and an old lady stepped out.

"We are very sorry," the children cried. "We are lost in the woods and have not eaten. We were just so hungry."

"Oh, you poor children," the old woman said kindly. "You must be tired and hungry. Come in and I will feed you."

She took their hands and led them into the house.

Lesson 19

Then, she placed platters of wonderful food in front of them. They ate until they could not eat any more. Then she gave them soft, comfortable beds to sleep in.

The old woman was only pretending to be kind.

Lesson 20

In truth, she built her candy and cake house to attract lost children. When she captured them she would fatten them up and then eat them, for she was really a wicked witch.

The next morning the witch crept into the room and carefully picked up Hansel without waking him. "He will be a tasty morsel," she mumbled gleefully to herself.

Lesson 21

Gretel was a much lighter sleeper than Hansel and had awaken when the evil witch crept into the room. Gretel heard the witch's words and realized she planned to eat Hansel. As soon as the witch exited the room with Hansel, Gretel quietly got out of bed and followed her. The witch went down some stairs and placed Hansel in a cage.

Lesson 22

Fearing the mean witch would catch her, Gretel hurried back up the stairs and into her bed.

When the witch came to fetch her a few moments later, Gretel pretended to be asleep.

"Come, girl, and help me bake the bread for the day," the old woman ordered. Gretel got up and followed the witch to the kitchen.

Lesson 23

"I have already heated the stove and kneaded the dough for the bread," said the witch. "Crawl in the oven and see if it is properly heated."

Gretel understood then that the witch intended to eat them both. So, now she had to save herself before she could save Hansel.

"I do not understand. I cannot fit in there," she said to the witch.

Lesson 24

"Of course you can. Just squeeze right in," replied the witch.

Gretel made a show of trying to figure out how to fit into the oven again. "No, it's much too small."

"Silly child. Even I can fit inside," the witch exclaimed, climbing in with inpatients to show Gretel. Gretel Hastily pushed the witch in, slammed the iron oven door and fastened the bolt.

Lesson 25

"Let me out!" the witch screamed, but Gretel ran away to free Hansel. She opened the door leading to the lower level and ran down the stairs. She grabbed the key hanging on the wall and quickly freed Hansel.

"What happened to the witch?" Hansel asked.

Lesson 26

"I locked her in the oven," Gretel answered.

"Let's hurry and get away from here," cried Hansel grabbing his sister's hand. The children stopped only long enough to fill their pockets and Gretel's apron with food. Then, they fled into the forest.

Lesson 27

The children walked for hours and hours. Finally they stopped to take a rest and have a bite to eat along a river bank.

"I believe I know this river," Hansel said. "I think it leads to our home."

The children set out again following the river.

Lesson 28

Sure enough, the forest began to look familiar. And after a long walk their house came into view.

The children ran into the house and into the arms of their father. He cried with relief and demanded to know where they had been all of this time.

Lesson 29

The children told him of how they'd been led into the forest and left behind twice. They told him of how they'd found their way back the first time with the stones. Then, they explained that the second time the birds and wild animals had eaten their bread trail.

"That is curious," their father said thoughtfully, scratching his chin.

Lesson 30

He told them that their step mother had returned home that day and baked wonderful treats that same evening. She told him that the children had run into the forest and she would bring them treats to try and get them to come home. She'd baked cakes and candies and then set out with her treats to look for them, but she never returned. And, they never saw her again.

www.ingramcontent.com/pod-product-compliance
Lightning Source LLC
Chambersburg PA
CBHW080535030426
42337CB00023B/4741